Inference

Activities

For Ages 8-12

David Newman

A Friendly Reminder

© David Newmonic Language Games 2013 - 2016

This book and all its contents are intellectual property.

No part of this publication may be stored in a retrieval system, transmitted or reproduced in any way, including but not limited to digital copying and printing without the prior agreement and written permission of the author.

However, I do give permission for class teachers or speech-language pathologists to print and copy individual worksheets for student use.

ISBN-13: 978-1490336589

ISBN-10: 1490336583

Contents

Introduction

Chapter One

What is Inference?

Inference is being conscious and aware of implied information. It is an essential part of understanding text, both fiction and non-fiction text.

To infer is the ability to unlock hidden information from written text. The reader is required to go deeper than the literal surface level of text and discover for themselves what the author doesn't state explicitly, but instead hints at. Inference skill is a crucial part of reading comprehension. If a child's inference skills are poor then it's a fair bet that their implicit understanding of what they read will also be poor. Most children can readily answer literal type questions about a text, but often struggle with information that is not specific and direct.

Authors of both fiction and nonfiction texts will actively engage their readers using a variety of techniques. This involves captivating their audience using images that spark readers' imaginations. One of the key elements on which an author relies, is that the reader has the ability to infer the implied or hidden information that is presented.

Please examine these two pieces of text, which present essentially the same information, and note the differences.

One: 'The aircraft's engines roared. As the pilot took off from the carrier's deck and guided the jet into the sky, he looked back and watched as the ship became smaller and smaller.'

Inference Activities

Two: 'The twin flames roared and the pilot gave the beast full throttle. He was soon airborne. Within moments the large gray brick of the flight deck receded and became simply a dot on the ocean's surface.'

Sentence one uses literal information to communicate a pilot taking off from the deck of an aircraft carrier. The language is direct and to the point, but perhaps a little bland.

In **sentence two** most of the information is implied. It relies on the reader's ability to infer that the language used - lithe beast, gray brick of the flight deck and a dot on the ocean's surface - is skilfully painting a picture of an aircraft taking off from the deck of an aircraft carrier.

Sentence two uses more elaborate language to create a complex and compelling image. However, it does rely on the reader to be able to connect all the dots and make sense of the imagery. Generally children with poor reading comprehension skills have difficulty connecting the dots, often due to poor vocabulary knowledge and poor inference skills.

The aim of the **Inference Activities** book is for your students to have practice engaging with highly interesting images and text, and thinking about the hidden information in each scenario. By practicing their inference skills your students will also improve their overall comprehension, and strengthen their written language skills.

What's in the Inference Activities Book?

Picture and Text

Sentence level Inference

Paragraph Level Inference – Nonfiction & Fiction

Text level Inference – Nonfiction & Fiction

Picture and Text

This section contains pictures with a caption and 3 questions each.

Sentence Level Inference

This section features 5 categories: *location, time, what, who,* and *why.*

Paragraph Level Inference

There are 10 individual chapters devoted to the paragraph level scenarios. Five are nonfiction - History, Weather, Plants, Solar System and Animal Kingdom. Five are fiction – Science Fiction & Fantasy, Adventure, Myths & Legend, Whimsy, and Kid's Stuff.

Text Level Inference – Nonfiction & Fiction

The section features a nonfiction news article and part of a fantasy story

. Using the Inference Activities Book

Recommended Book Sequence

Explain to your student/s what inference is – i.e. that it is hidden information that relies on us thinking about the author's message in new ways.

Sentence section: read the model sentence and discuss the meaning of the answer. Encourage your students to search for critical words in each sentence. Each sentence and paragraph will have critical words that rely on the reader using their background knowledge to connect the dots and understand the passage.

Paragraph Sections: Work through the paragraphs section at your leisure. Give as much guidance and assistance as possible. One paragraph level scenario per session is recommended. Discuss all responses and consult with the answer section in the appendix when needed.

Teacher Notes:

The questions can be read to students who can either answer orally or they can write their responses onto the printed worksheets. Answers to all of the questions can be found in the **appendix/answer** section.

Inference from

Pictures and Text

Chapter Two

Inference from Pictures and Text

'We flew to the ruined and deserted city'

a.   Why is the caption of the picture *'The ruined and deserted city*?'

    Answer: _____

b.   Would the plane have difficulty landing? How do you know that?

    Answer: _____

c.   Would it be cold flying an airplane with an open cockpit?

    Answer: _____

Inference from Pictures and Text

'When the ship's captain looked through the telescope at the

fast approaching vessel, he gasped in fear.'

a.   Who would be sailing on this ship? How do you know that?

   Answer: _____

b.   Why might the captain have gasped in fear?

   Answer: _____

c.   Is this scenario from modern times or from the past? How do you know that?

   Answer: _____

Inference from Pictures and Text

'I got the shock of my life when the train left the tracks and became airborne.'

a.   Why did the character get *the shock of his life*?

Answer: _____

b.   Is this scenario science fiction or real life? How do you know that?

Answer: _____

c.   Why don't trains have wings?

Answer: _____

Inference from Pictures and Text

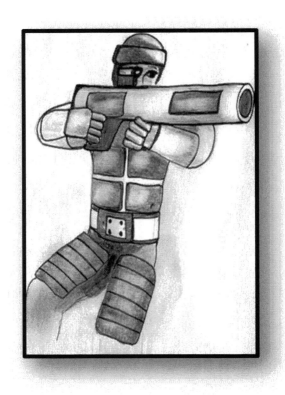

'The space trooper calmly looked through his range finder. The fierce alien warriors were right behind him.'

a.   Is the space trooper in any danger? How do you know that?

   Answer: _____

b.   Where does the space trooper work?

   Answer: _____

c.   Is the space trooper confident in his abilities? How do you know that?

   Answer: _____

Inference from Pictures and Text

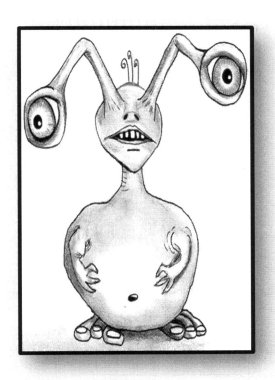

"Take me to your leader," said the creature'

a.   Does this creature have good vision? How do you know that?

   Answer: _____

b.   Is the creature from Earth? How do you know that?

   Answer: _____

c.   Would the creature come from an environment where vision was important to survival? How do you know that?

   Answer: _____

Inference from Pictures and Text

'Peter expertly launched the rocket and was thrilled with its

speed and power.'

a.   Is Peter having fun? How do you know that?

   Answer: _____

b.   Is Peter up high? How do you know that?

   Answer: _____

c.   Is Peter in control of the rocket? How do you know that?

   Answer: _____

Inference from Pictures and Text

'I needed to get the clothes off the clothesline. I didn't have much time.'

a   What is about to happen here?

Answer: _____

b.   Why does the character need to get the clothes off the clothesline?

Answer: _____

c.   Why might the character not have much time?

Answer: _____

Inference from Pictures and Text

'Adam had been warned to never sit in grandpa's chair.

Now it was too late.'

a.   Why had Adam been warned to never sit in the chair?

Answer: _____

b.   Why is it *too late*?

Answer: _____

c.   Is Adam still in his grandfather's house? How do you know that?

Answer: _____

Inference from Pictures and Text

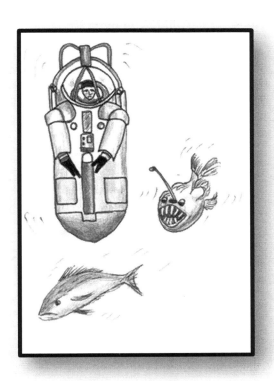

'When Captain Perry felt water trickling over his toes, he knew he was in trouble. He pushed the 'to surface' button.'

a. Where is Captain Perry?

Answer: _____

b. Why did Captain Perry hit the *'to surface'* button?

Answer: _____

c. Is Captain Perry in shallow water? How do you know that?

Answer: _____

Inference from Pictures and Text

'Kathy leaned forward and guided Saladin over. Only one obstacle to go and the gold medal was hers.'

a.   Who or what is Saladin?

   Answer: _____

b.   Is Kathy in a competition? How do you know that?

   Answer: _____

c.   Why did Kathy *lean forward*?

   Answer: _____

Sentence Level

Inference

Chapter three

Sentence Level Inference

Concept: Location

Location refers to being able to surmise where something or a person *is* from implied information. Location is suggestive of where someone or something is in an environment.

Example: Peter paddled his canoe skilfully between the big rocks.

Question: Where is Peter?

Answer: Peter is paddling his canoe down a river.

Critical Information: The important words here are *canoe, paddle* and *rocks*. We can image Peter guiding his canoe with his paddle between rocks on a fast flowing river.

Inference Exercises: Location

One: *The passenger jet*

The passenger jet landed and taxied to the arrival gate, and the people got off the plane.

Question: *Where* is the passenger jet?

Two: *The lion's cage*

Sasha walked past the lion's cage to the giraffe enclosure.

Inference Activities

Question: *Where* is Sasha?

Three: *The mountain goat*

The mountain goat stood upon a steep, snow covered ledge and looked down at the valley far below.

Question: *Where* is the mountain goat?

Four: *The penguin*

The penguin leapt out of the water and landed on the icy ground.

Question: *Where* is the penguin?

Five: *The pilot*

The pilot flipped on the switch and the mighty jet engines roared to life.

Question: *Where* is the pilot?

Six: *Katy*

Katy turned on the engine and buckled her seat belt.

Question: *Where* is Katy?

Seven: *Maths problem*

Paul watched his teacher write the solution to the maths problem.

Question: *Where* is Paul?

Eight: *Fishing*

Brendan cast his fishing line into the swiftly flowing water and watched

the fishermen on the opposite bank.

Question: *Where* is Brendan?

Nine: *Chlorinated water*

Catherine waded through the chlorinated water to the deep end, where

the big kids swam.

Question: *Where* is Catherine?

Ten: *Dr Benson*

Carl sat uneasily in the chair as Dr Benson inspected his teeth and

prepared the filling.

Question: *Where* is Carl?

Eleven: *Popcorn*

Susan sat in her seat, ate popcorn and waited for the movie to start.

Question: *Where* is Susan?

Twelve: *The children*

The children played outside until the bell rang and they had to line up.

Question: *Where* are the children?

Sentence Level Inference

Concept: Time

Time refers to being able to surmise when something occurs.

Example: Tyler finished his breakfast and walked to the bus station.

Question: What time of the day is it likely to be?

Answer: Early morning, probably about 8:00 – 8:30am.

Critical Information: The important words here are *breakfast* and *bus station*. The word breakfast suggests it's early morning and that Tyler needs to catch a bus to school.

Inference Exercises: Time

One: *Ice-cream*

It was a warm day and the ice-cream melted and dripped over the cone onto Chloe's hand.

Question: Had Chloe been holding the ice-cream cone long? What tells us this?

Two: *The sun*

The first rays of the sun were just starting to peek over the horizon.

Question: Is this describing early morning or late afternoon?

Three: *The bell*

The bell went and Chris walked to the school bus for the trip home.

Question: What time of day is it likely to be?

Four: *The sun*

The last of the sun's rays disappeared over the horizon and the air became cooler.

Question: Is this scene describing early morning or early evening? What tells us this?

Five: *Carl's soup*

Carl waited until his soup was cool enough to eat.

Question: Approximately (roughly) how long did Carl wait to eat his soup?

Six: *The post office*

Kim had a coffee in the café while she waited for the post office to open.

Question: What time of day was it likely to have been?

Seven: *The Christmas tree*

Dad put up the Christmas tree, while I draped the tree with tinsel and decorations.

Question: What part of the year is it likely to be?

Inference Activities

Eight: *The moon*

The moon was high in the sky and the stars shone brightly when Karen went swimming.

Question: Is Karen swimming in the morning or in the evening?

Nine: *The milk*

The milk on the stove boiled and frothed over the top of the saucepan and caused a mess.

Question: Approximately (roughly) for how long was the milk allowed to cook on the stove?

Ten: *Pam's school day*

Before Pam ventured out to go to school, she made certain that she had on her coat, mittens, scarf and beanie.

Question: Which season is it most likely to be?

Eleven: *The shadows*

The shadows grew longer as the sun went down, and the heat started to go out of the day.

Question: What part of the day is it likely to be?

Sentence Level Inference

Concept: What

What refers to what is happening or has happened, and what someone is or is doing.

Example: On the vessel's highest mast was a black flag with white skull and crossbones.

Question: What type of vessel is being described?

Answer: An old pirate ship

Critical Information: Highest mast, skull and crossbones.

Inference Exercises: What

One: *The captain*

The captain announced over the intercom that all passengers needed to fasten their seatbelts and prepare for landing.

Question: What type of transport were the passengers on?

Two: *The riders*

As Peter glanced over his shoulder at the other riders, his foot slipped off one of the pedals and he nearly toppled over.

Question: What nearly toppled over?

Inference Activities

Three: *The monkeys*

We could hear the monkeys chattering in their enclosure and lions roaring as we excitedly walked through the entrance.

Question: What is the entrance leading to?

Four: *Sunscreen*

The sand was hot under Tom's feet as he applied sunscreen to the areas not covered by his wetsuit.

Question: What is Tom putting sunscreen on?

Five: *Mars*

Ian adjusted the view on the lens, and, as if by magic, the planet Mars could clearly be seen through the eyepiece.

Question: What was Ian using to view the planet Mars?

Six: *The mountain*

The very top of the mountain blew off, and with a tremendous roar gases, ash, and smoke soared high into the sky.

Question: What is being described?

Seven: *The camel*

The camel walked over hot, baked rock and sand for over a week before it reached water.

Question: What type of place is the camel walking in?

Eight: *The archaeologist*

The archaeologist chipped away at the edge of the bone's outline in the rock, and carefully brushed off dust and dirt.

Question: What is the archaeologist chipping away at?

Nine: *The boy*

The boy peeled the yellow skin off the fruit and ate the soft flesh.

Question: What type of fruit is the boy eating?

Ten: *The insect*

The small creature skillfully spun its sticky trap and caught the insect.

Question: What small creature is being described?

Eleven: *Jasper*

Jasmine put one foot into the stirrup and swung her other leg other Jasper's high and broad back, and then sat tall in the saddle.

Question: What is Jasper?

Twelve: *The captain's orders*

The captain ordered all hatches secured and prepare to dive

Question: What type of vessel is being described?

Sentence Level Inference

Concept: Who

Who refers to what a person does for a living or who they may be related to.

Example: The man carefully washed and cleaned the wound and set the cast on the boy's broken leg.

Question: Who is the man? What does he do for a living?

Answer: The man is a medical doctor.

Critical Information: cleaned the wound, set the cast.

Inference Exercises: Who

One: *The driver's license*

The man pulled over my father's car and checked his driver's license.

Question: Who is the man? What does he do for a living?

Two: *The baby*

The woman fed and burped the baby and placed the sleepy girl in her cot.

Question: Who is the woman?

Three: *Miss Morris*

Miss Morris told me to pay attention while she worked out the mathematical problem on the whiteboard.

Question: Who is Miss Morris?

Four: *Jason*

Jason read the new order from the waiter, cooked the steak on both sides and prepared the sauce.

Question: Who is Jason?

Five: *Mr Harris*

One night the electricity in the house shut down and we had to call in Mr Harris to restore the power.

Question: Who is Mr Harris? What does he do for a living?

Six: *Jessica*

Jessica checked the patient's daily observation chart and adjusted his bandages.

Question: Who is Jessica? What does she do for a living?

Seven: *Phillip's drive*

Phillip started the vehicle's engine and got set for the long drive interstate in the 18 wheeler.

Question: Who is Phillip? What does he do for a living?

Inference Activities

Eight: *Natasha*

Natasha was expert at styling and cutting hair.

Question: Who is Natasha?

Nine: *The red truck*

Jesse bounded up the red truck's ladder through the smoke and prepared to turn the hose on.

Question: Who is Jesse? What does he do for a living?

Ten: *Mr Martin*

Mr Martin steered the long heavy vehicle through traffic into the station and opened the doors to let new passengers on.

Question: Who is Mr Martin? What does he do for a living?

Eleven: *The cows*

Andrew opened the gate to allow the cows to file through to the milking sheds.

Question: Who is Andrew? What does he do for a living?

Twelve: *The ticket*

Helen noticed that the car's parking pass had expired so she stuck a ticket to the car's windscreen.

Question: Who is Helen?

Sentence Level Inference

Concept: Why

Why refers to the reason an event occurred or the cause and effect of something.

Example: The strong wind filled the sails and the sailboat picked up speed.

Question: Why did the boat pick up speed?

Answer: Because the strong wind filled the sails.

Critical Information: strong wind, sail, speed.

Inference Exercises: Why

One: *The farmer*

The farmer couldn't find any sheep in the paddock and then noticed that someone had left the gate open.

Question: Why did the sheep get out of the paddock?

Two: *Covered in white*

It fell silently throughout the night and the next morning the ground was covered in white.

Inference Activities

Question: Why was the ground covered in white?

Three: *The DVD player*

Julie read the instructions of her new DVD player twice before she realized it wasn't yet plugged in.

Question: Why was the DVD player not working?

Four: *The pool*

Jenny held her breath before she dived in at the deep end of the pool.

Question: Why did Julie hold her breath?

Five: *The stadium*

Each time the home team scored a goal, a huge cheer filled the stadium.

Question: Why did the crowd cheer?

Six: *The storm*

After the fierce storm blew over, the power lines lay across the road.

Question: Why were the power lines across the road?

Seven: *The cat*

The dog barked when the cat jumped over the neighbor's fence onto the shed roof.

Question: Why did the dog bark?

Eight: *Adam's bike*

Adam got off his bike and pulled the bike pump off the frame and attached it to the front tire.

Question: Why did Adam get off his bike?

Nine: *The lawn mower*

The grass in the backyard was very long, so Paul started up the lawn mower.

Question: Why did Paul start the lawn mower?

Ten: *The oven*

Scott peered through the smoke, rapidly turned the oven off and opened the windows.

Question: Why did Scott open the windows?

Eleven: *The girl in the pool*

When the girl got out of the pool she quickly wrapped a towel around herself and shivered.

Question: Why did the girl quickly wrap a towel around herself?

Twelve: *The chef*

When the chef taste-tested the stew he grimaced and shook his head.

Question: Why did the chef grimace when he tasted the stew?

Paragraph Level

Inference *Fiction*

Chapter Four

Paragraph Level Fiction: *Science Fiction & Fantasy*

The following exercises focus on identifying inference at paragraph level. The exercises are examples of fiction, which have passages that rely on readers to inference or discover seemingly hidden information.

Example: The captain hammered down hard on the ship's controls. The large, elegant craft arced through the air and levelled out splendidly. Its silver panels rippled violently as the ship was buffeted by the blue planet's atmosphere, but it absorbed the shock easily. Far below, the huge continent of Africa peeped out beneath the white clouds and the captain smiled in satisfaction.

Question 1: Is the ship the type that floats on the water? How do you know that?

Answer: No. The ship is some type of spacecraft that is entering a planet's atmosphere.

Critical Information: *buffeted by the atmosphere, peeped down through the clouds, arced through the air.*

Question 2: What is the name of the blue planet? How do you know that?

Answer: Earth. The passage mentions Africa, which is a continent on Earth.

Critical Information: *blue planet, Africa.*

One: *The Rocket Pack*

Up I went. Up, up, up, to the very top. My legs ached and my arms trembled from the effort. The tower was over a mile high, its tall mast bathed in the moon's light. From up here I could see all the way to the ocean. Slowly, slowly, I dangled my legs over the edge and tightened the belt of the rocket pack strapped to my back. My heart thumped wildly as I flicked the on switch. The pulse of the rocket motors whirred to life and I prepared to launch myself.

Question 1: Is the character climbing the tower at night?

Question 2: Does the character feel excited or fearful when he turns the motors on? How do you know that?

Two: *Spike*

It often drove the space cadet supervisor mad. There were 12 students in the supervisor's physical exercise class, 11 humans and Spike. The supervisor felt a twinge of annoyance whenever Spike used its multiple artificial limbs to complete the obstacle course, always in record time. The supervisor felt Spike had an unfair advantage. Spike completed the obstacle course in 10 minutes, half the time it took the human students.

Question 1: What is Spike? How do you know that?

Question 2: How long did the students take to complete the course?

Three: *The Vortex Creator*

As I entered the date, year and destination into the machine's computer, I noticed that I was still wearing the Roman soldier uniform. I needed to quickly change into the clothes of an 18th century pirate. I didn't have much time. Before I knew it, the machine's vortex creator opened a blue flamed, electrically charged time portal and I was launched onto my next trip.

Question 1: What type of machine is the character travelling on? How do you know that?

Question 2: Why does the character need to quickly change his clothes?

Inference Activities

Four: *The guards*

This was going to be hard. In the passage ahead of me were the fearsome alien guards. They were armed to the teeth, whereas all I had were my bare hands. I had to rely on my unarmed combat training to make it past them. There was no other way to get to my spaceship. I crouched down and raced down the passage, yelling wildly. The guards saw me and prepared to open fire but I was too quick for them.

Question 1: Was the character carrying any weapons? How do you know that?

Question 2: Why did the character need to confront the alien guards?

Five: *The brundle trumper*

I battled valiantly against it. On it came. Step after terrible step. I struggled and pushed my tough metal and plastic body against its massive bulk. The planet's most fierce predator, the *brundle trumper,* towered over me. It howled in frustration as it snapped at my head's electrical circuits with its three sets of beastly jaws. I kept it at bay long enough for my master and lady to strap themselves into the shuttle and escape.

Question 1: Are the characters on Earth? How do you know that?

Question 2: How many heads might the brundle trumper have? How do you know that?

Six: *Prince Angus*

The castle courtyard was very quiet. Prince Angus felt a little shiver go up his spine as he walked across the abandoned castle grounds. He felt he was being watched by something hostile. He silently drew his sword from its sheath. Without warning, the scaly creature flew into the courtyard and launched its attack. Hot breath roared from its snout and engulfed the prince. Only his shield stopped the prince from being covered in flames.

Question 1: What type of mythical beast is the creature with the fiery breath?

Question 2: Do people live at the castle? How do you know that?

Seven: *Grunt*

It was a good plan. My apprentice, Grunt, snuck inside the tall chapel to open the doors from the inside. I waited anxiously while mounted upon faithful Jenson. Jenson's head tossed fitfully as I pulled back on the reins. He could sense my excitement. Not long now. Soon I would confront the evil lord Baleen and steal away his daughter, my fiancée, the Princess Chloe. The chapel gates opened. Jenson snorted and trotted forward with great purpose.

Question 1: What is Jenson? How do you know that?

Question 2: What is the character anxiously waiting for?

Inference Activities

Eight: *The angry farmer*

All the soup was spread across the floor. The grain had been eaten. Feathers left in the fireplace showed that the creature had flown down the chimney during the night, eaten the grain, tipped over the soup pot and flown back out again. The farmer was angry. He would have no soup to dunk his bread into at supper time. Tonight, he would set a trap and catch the thief once and for all.

Question 1: What might the thief be? How do you know that?

Question 2: Why is the farmer angry?

Nine: *The Mission*

'Grab the little devil, before it's too late,' bellowed the captain of the guards. There was no stopping me. I was too fast, too agile, too nimble for the bulky guards. They in their heavy armour with their wide girths, what chance did they have of catching me? Outside the gates, my master's army waited. I leapt upon the highest battlement and let loose an arrow at the lever that secured the gates. With a loud ping the lever snapped and the huge castle gates lurched slowly open. My mission was complete.

Question 1: What was the character's mission?

Question 2: What weapon was the character carrying with him?

Ten: *The wizard*

An electric bolt of pure energy smashed into my head. The force of the blast lifted my helmet clean off. I could dimly hear it clanging down the tower's steps. I groggily raised myself to my knees and tried to clear my mind. My head ached fiercely. I could taste the blood that trickled from my mouth. That was close! I was determined that the wizard would not get a second chance. I raised my shield, stood up once more, and bravely shuffled forward.

Question 1: What do you think the wizard did?

Question 2: What did the force of the magic blast do to the character? How do you know that?

Paragraph Level Fiction: *Myths*

One: *Prometheus (Greek Myth)*

Prometheus (Prom-eth-e-us), an immortal Titan, was a friend to mankind. Of all the Greek Titans, Prometheus was considered to be the most gifted. The kindly and generous Titan stole fire from Zeus's temple and gifted it to man. For stealing the fire, Zeus had Prometheus chained to a rock to endure the hot sun and the freezing cold for eternity.

Question 1: Was Prometheus a man? How do you know that?

Question 2: Was Zeus angry? How do you know that?

Two: *Pandora's Box (Greek Myth)*

The Greek god Zeus was furious at Prometheus (Prom-eth-e-us) for stealing fire from Mount Olympus. In revenge he sent to Earth, Pandora, a beautiful woman who became the wife of Prometheus' brother, Epimetheus (Ep-i-meth-e-us). Pandora was given a mysterious box and was told that she must never open it. Overcome by curiosity, Pandora opened the box and let loose into the world all of mankind's sufferings and misfortune.

Question 1: Was Pandora foolish to open the box?

Question 2: Why did Pandora open the box?

Three: *The Minotaur (Greek Myth)*

The Minotaur was a brutal and aggressive creature. It had the muscular body of a man and the head of a savage bull. The Minotaur was such a fearsome creature that the king of Crete, King Minos, constructed an extensive and complex labyrinth to contain it. The labyrinth was a maze of sharp twists and turns and obstacles. At its centre was the Minotaur. The monster was eventually killed by the Greek hero, Theseus.

Question 1: Why was the Minotaur dangerous?

Question 2: Why was the Minotaur difficult to find?

Four: *Thor (Norse Myth)*

Thor is the strongest of all Norse gods. Thor wears a belt that doubles his strength. He also wields a hammer which causes great noise and sparks with which to destroy his enemies. The great Norse god is associated with thunder and lightning, and the protection of mankind. Thursday is named after Thor.

Question 1: What would happen to Thor if he were to lose his belt?

Question 2: What might cause thunder and lightning, according to the Norse myth?

Inference Activities

Five: *Romulus and Remus (Roman Myth)*

The twin boys, Romulus and Remus, were born to their mother Rhea. Their uncle, for political reasons, kidnaps the infants and leaves them in a harsh environment to die. They are found by a kindly she-wolf who nurses and raises the twin boys. A shepherd later discovers them and raises the boys to adulthood. As adults, Romulus and Remus build the city of Rome.

Question 1: What may have happened to the infants if the she-wolf had not nursed them?

Question 2: What could a harsh environment mean?

Six: *Maui of a Thousand Tricks (Polynesian Myth)*

Maui, the trickster hero, decided that the sun moved across the sky too quickly and the days were too short. Maui cut his wife's long hair to create very tough rope. He then constructed and formed a noose from the rope and launched it at the sun. The sun was caught and could not struggle free. The sun can now only creep across the sky slowly and the days are longer.

Question 1: Could Maui create rope using short hair?

Question 2: Did Maui's plan work? How do you know that?

Seven: *Why the Crow is Black (Indigenous Australian Myth)*

One fine day a crow and a hawk hunted together. They decided to share the day's catch with each other. The crow had a good day and caught several ducks, but was greedy and ate all the birds. The hawk caught nothing. The hawk, angry at the crow, wrestled him near a campfire. The crow got rolled in the ashes and turned black. Since that time all crows have been black.

Question 1: Why was the hawk angry with the crow?

Question 2: Did the hawk hunt well? How do you know that?

Eight: *The Holy Grail (Celtic Myth)*

The Holy Grail is a mythical long lost sacred cup used by Jesus Christ at his last supper. In the Arthurian legend, the grail is a symbol of God's grace and available to those who are good of heart. King Arthur commanded his knights to find the Holy Grail. After many fruitless years of searching, Galahad, the most pure of knights, found the grail. According to legend, Galahad, filled with divine light, ascended to heaven holding the grail.

Question 1: Why was Galahad able to find the Holy Grail?

Question 2: Was the grail easy to find? How do you know that?

Inference Activities

Nine: *Heracles (Greek Myth)*

Heracles was a very strong Greek hero who was half man and half god. To become a god Heracles had to perform twelve labours. Heracles first task was to kill the Nemean lion, a fierce beast that had such thick skin that no weapon could pierce it. Both Heracle's sword and spear were ineffective against the lion, but he was able to strangle it with his bare hands.

Question 1: Why were the sword and spear ineffective?

Question 2: Why was Heracles able to strangle the lion?

Ten: *The Phoenix* (Chinese Myth)

The phoenix (fee-nicks) is a mythical bird with feathers that blend all the known colors. Its birdcall is a sweet harmony of five notes that is pleasing to the ear. It is thought that the phoenix bathes in the purest natural spring water that flows high in the mountains. The Chinese consider the appearance of the mythical phoenix as a sign of prosperity and wealth.

Question 1: Is the phoenix a real bird? How do you know that?

Question 2: Is the phoenix a colourful bird? How do you know that?

Paragraph Level Fiction: *Adventure*

One: *Top of the mast*

The captain ordered me to the top of the mast. The main sail needed to be secured. The wind howled and its sharp fingers scratched at my shirt, making it ripple fiercely. The waves pounded against the ship's wooden beams. Each wave thrust the ship to the side and the main mast shivered, nearly tossing me down into the violent swell of the ocean. I hung onto the mast for dear life, determined to do my job.

Question 1: What was the weather like? How do you know that?

Question 2: Is the character frightened? How do you know that?

Two: *Old Boxy*

The whole family from the homestead hurried over to see me ride Old Boxy. Everyone was here to watch the show. I carefully placed my left boot in the stirrup, lifted up and swung into the saddle. My heart beat so hard I thought I might faint. The brute stood motionless as I kicked with my heels. Then, with a malicious launch, the creature's back legs thrust out, and I was airborne and soon lying face first in the mud.

Question 1: What is Old Boxy? How do you know that?

Question 2: Is Old Boxy well known for being difficult to ride?

Inference Activities

Three: *The silver craft*

It was the most beautiful sight I had ever seen. The curved arc of the planet stretched out below me. And even though it was the middle of a bright, sunny day, I could see the twinkling of stars. I cut back on the huge engines and the sleek, silver craft coasted on the thin air of the upper atmosphere. The craft's wing tips caught the sun's rays and glinted. Far below, I could see oceans, countries, and continents as if they were part of a huge patchwork quilt.

Question 1: What type of craft is the pilot flying? How do you know that?

Question 2: Is the pilot high in the sky? How do you know that?

Four: *Rocketgirl*

Rocketgirl propelled herself through the air like a small rock released from a slingshot. Her hair streamed in the slipstream and her feet were a blur of motion. She was running faster than a bullet train and didn't slow or hesitate when she came to the mighty river. She jumped! Rocketgirl's speed and momentum launched her high and long. She touched down smoothly seconds later, a few feet past the opposite river bank, a distance of nearly a mile.

Question 1: Why were Rocketgirl's feet a blur of motion?

Question 2: Could Rocketgirl have made the jump if she had not been running quickly? How do you know that?

56

Five: *Climb to the summit*

I battled against it. Step by step I made my way up. There was no turning back. It was easier to go on than to retreat to the safety of the base camp. I dug into the ice with my pick and hauled myself up the rope. The wind howled savagely and whipped up ice and snow and flung it at me. My climbing gear protected me from the worst of it, but small slithers of ice found their way through and chilled my flesh. My fingers were blue when I made it to the summit.

Question 1: What is the character doing? How do you know that?

Question 2: Was it a cold environment? How do you know that?

Six: *Hidden*

Time was running out. My camera clicked and flashes of light briefly lit the darkness. A noise outside! I silently closed the file and hid beneath the desk as the door opened. Two guards entered. They muttered something in their language and flicked on the light switch. One of the guards had seen the flash of the camera beneath the door jamb. Despite all my training, I had been careless. They searched the room, but I was too well hidden.

Question 1: Was the character working in the dark? How do you know that?

Question 2: Does the character spy for a living? How do you know that?

Inference Activities

Seven: *Phantom*

I gently tapped Phantom's flanks with my heels and he broke into a canter. I sat up straight and sharp in the saddle. My hands held the reins firmly but gave Phantom enough slack so he could stretch out and shake his head. His neck arched majestically as he loped effortlessly across the field. A small command from me and Phantom broke into a gallop and thundered across the ground. I leant forward in the saddle and thrilled at Phantom's agility and power.

Question 1: Was Phantom going fast at the end of the passage? How do you know that?

Question 2: What is Phantom? How do you know that?

Eight: *The lost valley of Chixilbar*

We stopped when we reached the edge. The lost valley of Chixibar! There it was, far below us. The valley was in a huge basin shaped like a football field that stretched for 20 kilometres, east to west. Our small expedition had hacked and cut through the dense rainforest for 2 months, but we had made it. We lowered several lines of rope over the cliff face and started the long climb down. Loud cries and excited chattering from exotic species floated up from the valley with the breeze.

Question 1: Was the lost valley difficult to reach? How do you know that?

Question 2: What might 'exotic species' be referring to?

Nine: *Dive*

'Dive! Dive! Dive!' My hand fumbled as I urgently released the ballast tanks. The ship began its long descent. The captain barked orders to the crew. Our ship was in terrible danger. Above, on the water's surface, a naval ship hunted us. It launched its depth charges. The sonar operator cried out a warning, 'Brace for impact!' The depth charges exploded and a booming rush of water hit the ship's fragile hull. We continued to dive until we were out of danger.

Question 1: What type of ship is the crew in? How do you know that?

Question 2: Why did the crew need to brace for impact?

Ten: *The map*

Andrew followed the trail. The faded and stained map pointed to the right direction. He passed the rock shaped like a frog and walked through the tunnel formed by tree branches. At last, he reached the spot on the map marked by a cross - the valley of hard dirt. Andrew drove the shovel into the flinty ground lifting small chunks of soil. After 5 hours of back breaking labour, Andrew's shovel struck something hard and metallic.

Question 1: What type of map was Andrew following?

Question 2: Why was the digging described as back breaking labour?

Paragraph Level Fiction: *Whimsy*

One: *Take your medicine*

My grandmother tries to feed me fish oil. *'Omega 3, good for growing boys,'* she says. She pours it onto a spoon, *'Come boy, take your medicine.'* I back away as she laughs her terrible laugh. I feel as Hansel must have felt in the gingerbread house. I search for an exit. There! The kitchen door! I lunge. I am fast, but my grandmother is faster. Soon I am gagging as the wretched oil works its way down my throat.

Question 1: What is the boy inferring his grandmother is like?

Question 2: Did the boy make it out the kitchen door?

Two: *Uncle Angus*

Uncle Angus is the worst kind of tickler. After footy he holds me down and tickles while I squirm and laugh in desperation. Soon enough, after a few social graces are observed, he has me pinned. I try to escape but am not fast enough. Angus tickles my armpits. I can't help it. I want to yell *'Stop, Stop,'* but can't form the words from laughing so much.

Question 1: What could a few social graces be?

Question 2: Why can't the character escape Uncle Angus' tickling?

Three: *Proust*

Our cat, Proust, (Pr-oo-st) is a little bit mad. He likes to torment Jed, the neighbor's dog. Jed is big and tough, and would love to get his paws on Proust. There is a big wooden fence that separates our property from the neighbors. Proust's tactic is to scratch the wooden paling. Jed, attracted by the scratching, pokes his nose through a gap in the fence. Proust whacks Jed on the nose with his paw. Jed goes ballistic, but always pokes his nose through again. Whack, goes Proust once more. Jed's not too bright.

Question 1: Why is Jed described as *not too bright*?

Question 2: Why would Jed would love to get his paws on Proust?

Four: *The freezer*

Our freezer freezes everything until the freezer is one big block of ice. Dad said he'll fix it soon. But I'm not hopeful. He also said he'd fix the washing machine soon. That was three years ago. The clothes still come out three sizes smaller. Today, I have a problem. I need to get to my sausage rolls. They're in the freezer. I open the freezer door and know what I must do. I go to the shed and locate the pick axe. I swing and dig until clumps of ice cover the kitchen floor. I find my sausage rolls.

Question 1: What did the character mean by 'I know what I must do?'

Question 2: Was the washing machine fixed by the character's dad?

Inference Activities

Five: *The missing keys*

This was urgent. I had two minutes to find the house keys before my parents arrived. My bedroom was like a forest with a deep undergrowth of discarded clothes. The keys were in here somewhere, so I began the search. I looked under the tower of pizza boxes. Nothing! I picked up five pairs of jeans from the floor and checked their pockets. Again, nothing. Then I looked up. Something metallic was hanging from the ceiling light. I recognized them and breathed a sigh of relief.

Question 1: Why did the character breathe a sigh of relief?

Question 2: Was the character's bedroom messy?

Six: *Making puddles*

Above them the sky was turning dark and gloomy, but Sally was sure they could make it in time. Sally and her brother Peter scampered to the shops, which was at the end of the street. They were halfway to the supermarket when it came down. Sally and Peter walked into the supermarket, water dripping from their clothes, their hair, and their shoes. One of the staff offered the children a towel, but they said, 'No thanks.' Peter grinned and said that he liked making puddles.

Question 1: What happened to the children on the way to the supermarket?

Question 2: What did Sally think they could make in time?

Seven: *The jump*

Derek took a deep breath and leapt out of the narrow doorway and through the air. The wind whipped and rippled his jumpsuit as Derek tumbled through the air. He grasped the red cord and tugged it firmly. Above him the beautiful nylon billowed as it opened. Derek floated down through the air slowly and calmly.

Question 1: What was the doorway Derek was standing in?

Question 2: What was Derek doing?

Eight: *The dentist's waiting room*

The dentist's waiting room seems huge. I nervously sit in the chair. I want to disappear. There is no avoiding it. I will have to confront my deepest fear. My older brother Tommy loves to tease me. He knows of my fear because, in a moment of weakness, I told him. *'Soon Michael, soon,'* says Tommy. He punches my arm. Tommy says, *'I can hear the little motor now. I can hear it spinning. Imagine how it will feel when the Dentist starts up the drill. The sound it will make.'* Tommy laughs. I sink further into the chair.

Question 1: What is the character's deepest fear?

Question 2: Was it a good idea for Michael to tell Tommy about his deepest fear? How do you know that?

Inference Activities

Nine: *The new pyjamas*

My Aunt sent me new pyjamas for my birthday. My new pyjamas are a crazy lime green and are just what I am looking for. I bound up the stairs to my room and try them on. They are a perfect fit. I then slip on my green fluorescent (fl-oo-res-cent) sneakers and tie the laces. Two items remain. My cape is first. I tie it on and admire its dark green hues. Then, on goes the mask. I am ready. I am the Green Rocket. And I am ready to fight crime and battle evil doers.

Question 1: Does the character live in a two story house?

Question 2: Is the character a real superhero or just a child playacting?

Ten: *The bully*

The bully got on the bus. His eyes scanned the rows of seats and locked on mine. He smiled. The bully liked to steal my sandwiches. He loved my mother's homemade jam. Today would be different. My sandwiches concealed a secret weapon. Instead of jam the sandwiches were spread with Pedro's red hot, turbo charged chili sauce. The bully snatched my sandwiches from me, unwrapped one and took a large bite. He gasped. His face turned bright pink and his eyes bulged. The chili was working its magic.

Question 1: Did the bully know the sandwiches contained chili sauce?

Question 2: What does the chili was working its magic mean?

Paragraph Level Fiction: *Kid's stuff*

One: *Fish & chip night*

Ah, fish and chip night; the most glorious night of the week. My family embraces the humble chip, and its partner, fried fish. An explosion of flavor in my mouth, as the first chip touches my tongue. I start with one, held between my thumb and index finger. One becomes two; two soon progresses to become a handful at a time.

Question 1: Does the first chip taste nice? How do you know that?

Question 2: What is the character holding a whole handful of at a time?

Two: *The brush*

It was time to leave. My older teenage sisters were fighting over who had used Jasmine's hairbrush. Jasmine had found dog hair in it. She asked Karen if she had used the brush to brush the dog's hair. Karen scoffed. It was only a matter of time before the finger of blame swung onto me. And it wasn't really my fault, was it? Yesterday, the dog's coat was tatty and I used the first thing I could find.

Question 1: Why might the character think it was time to leave?

Question 2: Did the character use his sister's hairbrush to brush the dog's hair? How do you know that?

Inference Activities

Three: *All the colors of the rainbow*

They were all so mouth-watering. There they sat, in their little tubs. All the colors of the rainbow and even colors I could not name. And there were many different flavors to try. There was such an abundance of sweetness and goodness that I scarcely knew where to start. I scanned the contents of the glass freezer and made my selection. I pointed to the strawberry and chocolate flavors. The attendant scooped the stuff into a waffle cone.

Question 1: What is the character about to buy? How do you know that?

Question 2: Were there more than two flavors on offer? How do you know that?

Four: *The large vehicle*

I scrambled after the large vehicle. It had to make a stop on Western Avenue, so I knew I would get one opportunity. If I didn't manage to catch it at the next stop, I would be late for school. I ran so hard I thought my lungs would burst. With a final lunge I pushed through the doors and paid the driver my fare. I had made it.

Question 1: What is the large vehicle?

Question 2: What was the character referring to when he/she stated, 'I knew I had chance?'

Five: *Grandma's apple pie*

I remember Grandma's apple pie. Grandma was raised during the war years. It was a time when food was scarce. She was taught to never waste food. Grandma would always put the whole apple into her pies: the core, the pips, stem – everything. As I ate her pie, I waited for that horrible moment when a piece of apple core got stuck between my teeth or I crunched on a hard pip.

Question 1: Why did Grandma put the whole apple into her pies?

Question 2: Does the character enjoy eating Grandma's apple pie? How do you know that?

Six: *The dice roll*

All I needed was a 3 or more on the dice roll and I would win. My friend and I had been playing the game for what seemed an age. In the final moments of the game, I was just ahead. It had all come down to the final dice roll. If I rolled a 3, 4, 5, or 6 the game was mine and I would be the victor. The odds were on my side. I rolled the dice. The number staring up at me was a 2. My friend gave a triumphant cheer as I slumped to the floor in defeat.

Question 1: Had the children been playing the game for long? How do you know that?

Question 2: Why were the odds on the character's side?

Inference Activities

Seven: *The cold floor*

It was midnight. I counted the chimes from the old grandfather clock in the lounge room. I had to go to the bathroom but knew I had to confront the long dark of the hallway. The hall light bulb had blown and had not been replaced. With an extreme effort I threw off the quilt cover and stood up. The hardwood floor was as cold as the arctic. I quickly paced down the hallway and groaned when I banged into the sideboard. Ouch! I groped forward and clicked on the switch in the bathroom. I was suddenly bathed in light.

Question 1: How did the character know it was midnight?

Question 2: Why did the character bang into the sideboard?

Eight: *The diving board*

I felt very small. I was psyching myself to dive off the highest diving board in the state. All the other kids were lined up behind me. They were impatient. They bawled at me to jump. I had to do something. I walked pigeon-toed to the edge and looked down. Big mistake! I felt dizzy and nearly fainted. But I had made my decision. I closed my eyes and leapt through the air. I splashed into the pool's water a few moments later.

Question 1: Why was it a big mistake to look over the edge?

Question 2: Why were the other children impatient?

Nine: *Thirst*

I was near mad from thirst and still only fifth in line. We had one drink fountain at school and Ken was taking forever. We had just finished playing football and my clothes stuck to my skin from sweat. The sun beat down on my head as I watched Ken slowly, oh so slowly, gulp down what seemed enough water to fill a bath. Ken finally finished and the next wretched boy drank slowly as well.

Question 1: Is the character next in line for a drink?

Question 2: Why does the character refer to the next boy as 'wretched?'

Ten: *Auntie's dinner*

My big brother has a talent for saying the wrong thing at the wrong time. Yesterday, we were at my Auntie's house for dinner. He picked up something odd from his plate and said, *"What on Earth is this?"* My mother gasped and looked at her sister apologetically. My Aunt, not one to take any nonsense from kids, said, *"It's cucumber from my garden, boy, and you'll eat it and like it."* My brother went red in the face and ate the cucumber in silence.

Question 1: Did the Aunt buy the cucumber from the supermarket? How do you know that?

Question 2: Why did the mother gasp?

Paragraph Level
Inference *Non-Fiction*

Chapter Five

Paragraph Level Non Fiction: *History*

The following exercises focus on identifying inference at paragraph level. The exercises are examples of expository text (non-fiction) which typically relies on readers to inference hidden information.

Example: *In the old city of Istanbul, atop a hill, rests the Hagia Sophia, an ancient Christian church. The queue of tourists to see the Hagia Sophia is sometimes several hundred metres long.*

Question 1: Is the Hagia Sophia very old? How do you know that?

Question 2: Is the Hagia Sophia a popular tourist attraction? How do you know that?

Answer: The Hagia Sophia is described as ancient, so it is very old. We can describe it as a tourist attraction because of long queues of tourists.

Inference Exercises: Paragraph Level - History

One: *Henry Ford*

Henry Ford was the first to mass produce motor cars on an assembly line. He did this with the popular Ford Model T car between 1908 and 1927. The car was both cheap to buy and run.

Question 1: Were motor cars mass produced before 1908? How do you know that?

Question 2: Why was the Ford Model T a popular car?

Inference Activities

Two: *Napoleon*

Napoleon Bonaparte's armies were defeated at the battle of Waterloo in 1815. Despite his armies many victories in past years, the defeat at Waterloo shattered the French emperor's power. After the battle, Napoleon was sent into exile to the tiny island of St Helena, where he died a few years later.

Question 1: Had Napoleon's armies been successful before the battle of Waterloo? How do you know that?

Question 2: Did Napoleon rule France after 1815?

Three: *Gutenberg*

The first printing press was invented by Johannes Gutenburg in the year 1440. The printing press changed civilization by enabling many books to be printed quickly and easily. Before Gutenburg's invention, book printing relied on copying hand written sheets of paper, which was slow and difficult.

Question 1: Why do you think the printing press was such an important invention?

Question 2: Why do you think printing was slow and difficult before Gutenburg's invention?

Four: *The Rosetta stone*

The Rosetta stone provided the key to successfully translating ancient Egyptian writing. The stone had the same text in three ancient languages carved into it: Greek, Demotic and Egyptian. A clever translator was able to use the known written language of Greek to unlock the Egyptian writing code.

Question 1: Before the discovery of the Rosetta stone, were translators successful in understanding ancient Egyptian writing?

Question 2: Why was the translator clever?

Five: *Greek houses*

Ancient Greek houses were small and generally had two storeys. Some houses had dirt floors, whereas others had stone floors. Windows were tiny and up high and let in little sunlight. There was very little furniture, and indoor fires made the house smoky and difficult to breathe in.

Question 1: Would the inside of an ancient Greek home be dark or filled with light? How do you know this?

Question 2: By modern standards, would an ancient Greek house be a comfortable place to live?

Inference Activities

Six: *The stirrup*

Ancient warfare took a leap forward in about 700 CE with the invention of the stirrup. Before the stirrup was attached to the saddle, cavalry would fall off their horses if they wore heavy armour. The stirrup allowed cavalry to move more effectively while carrying heavy weapons and shields.

Question 1: Why did cavalry troops wearing heavy armour fall of their horses before the invention of stirrups?

Question 2: Why were cavalry troops able to move more easily with the addition of the stirrup attached to the saddle?

Seven: *First written language*

The ancient Sumerians were the first to develop a written language. They wrote thin wedges and symbols onto soft clay that would later harden into very tough clay tablets. Their skill in writing helped the Sumerians develop long distance trade with other countries.

Question 1: Why do you think we in modern times are able to unearth and read ancient Sumerian writing?

Question 2: Why do you think the Sumerian's were able to increase trade after they had discovered written language?

Eight: *Marco Polo*

Marco Polo was an Italian merchant who travelled from Venice to China in the 13th century – about 700 years ago. It took Marco Polo over three years to travel the Silk Road from Italy to China on foot - a distance of about 4000 kilometres. In the 13th century, there were many bandits along the Silk Road, so people often travelled in large groups.

Question 1: Why do you think it took Marco Polo so many years to travel to China from Italy?

Question 2: Why do you think people travelled in large groups on the Silk Road?

Nine: *The French Revolution*

The French Revolution started in 1789. France was governed by an uncaring king who ruled the people as he pleased. The king wanted to raise taxes on all the poor citizens, but not the wealthy citizens. The poor citizens of France had had enough and overthrew the French king and his nobles.

Question 1: Why had the French citizens had enough of the king?

Question 2: What tells us the king was uncaring?

Inference Activities

Ten: *The Titanic*

The Titanic was a large and impressive ocean liner that could carry up to 2000 passengers and was claimed to be unsinkable. The Titanic was on its maiden (first) voyage in 1912 across the Atlantic Ocean when it struck an iceberg and sank.

Question 1: Was the Titanic unsinkable? How do you know that?

Question 2: How many voyages did Titanic complete?

Paragraph Level Non-Fiction: *Weather*

One: *Temperature*

A thermometer measures the warmth of the air. The most comfortable temperature for people to live in is usually 20-25 degrees Celsius, or 68-77 degrees Fahrenheit. When the temperature drops below 20 degrees Celsius it is more likely that people will wear more clothes. At temperatures above 25 degrees, people will like to be near water.

Question 1: Why do you think people would wear more clothes when the temperature is below 20 degrees Celsius?

Question 2: Why would people want to be near water at temperatures above 25 degrees Celsius?

Two: *Fog*

Fog can be very difficult to see through. Fog is made up of millions of tiny droplets of water that absorb sound, and make vision quite difficult. If heavy fog occurs on a busy freeway, drivers have to slow down. Driving a car quickly through dense fog will soon lead to accidents.

Question 1: Would it be easy to hear clearly in a dense fog?

Question 2: Why would driving a car quickly through thick fog be dangerous?

Inference Activities

Three: *Clouds*

Cumulonimbus (cum-ul-on-im-bus) clouds are storm clouds. They resemble gigantic skyscrapers in the sky. These clouds stretch high in the sky for many thousands of meters and the air within is dynamic and moves very fast. Very large raindrops, thunder, lightning and hailstones are a feature of thunderclouds such as these. It's a good idea to stay inside when these clouds approach.

Question 1: Why are cumulonimbus clouds compared to giant skyscrapers?

Question 2: Why would you stay indoors when storm clouds approach?

Four: *Thunder*

Thunder occurs when lightning heats the air around it. The rapid increase of heat sends shock waves through the air. The long, loud, deep rumbling sound that thunder produces is shock waves bumping along the bottom of clouds and rebounding to the Earth's surface. The sound of thunder can sometimes wake you when you sleep.

Question 1: Does thunder occur before or after lightning flashes?

Question 2: Why does thunder sometimes wake sleeping people?

Five: *Snow*

Snow is formed in the highest and coldest parts of clouds. Snowflakes are created when ice crystals form around a tiny piece of dust. Ice crystals form a variety of unique patterns and are very light. They swirl high in clouds driven by cold winds. The crystals eventually become big enough and heavy enough that they fall to earth as snow – a snowflake.

Question 1: Why do ice crystals not fall to earth immediately?

Question 2: What might happen to ice crystals that got swirled around in warm winds?

Six: *Cyclone*

A cyclone is a devastating tropical storm. Cyclones begin as a typical thunderstorm but rapidly develop into monster storms with winds of over 100 kilometres per hour. Cyclones are driven by the heat offered from warm ocean currents and need this warmth to fuel their power. Cyclones cannot form over land, or continue over land for very long.

Question 1: What might happen to a house that got hit by winds of over 100 kilometres per hour?

Question 2: Why would a cyclone struggle to exist over land?

Inference Activities

Seven: *Drought*

Drought can make entire countries desolate, and the absence of water can cause havoc to plants and animals. In areas where there are large open spaces that rely on water, animals can quickly die if the drought lingers for too long. In severe drought, dead grass causes the soil to blow away in hot winds.

Question 1: Why would soil blow away if no grass were in the ground?

Question 2: Why would the absence of water be disastrous for many plants and animals?

Eight: *Weather*

The weather is a term we use to describe how warm or cold the day is. Weather is very changeable. Atmospheric conditions can be very hard to predict, even for weather forecasting experts. For instance, months of heavy rain can follow an extended period of drought, or cold weather can interrupt a previously warm, sunny day.

Question 1: Why do forecasting experts have difficulty predicting weather day by day?

Question 2: Should you bring along a jumper on a warm, sunny day if the forecaster says to expect rain?

Nine: *Rain*

Water vapor is an invisible gas that forms tiny water droplets. The tiny water droplets condense together to form clouds. When the water droplets become larger they fall through the air as rain. If the air in the clouds is very cold, then the water freezes into lumps of ice, called hailstones.

Question 1: Would rain fall from clouds if water droplets remained tiny?

Question 2: If hail falls from the sky would the air in the clouds be cold? How do you know that?

Ten: *Tornados*

A tornado, also known as a twister, is a violent swirling tube of air that sucks up debris and causes extensive damage to everything it touches. It is very dangerous to be caught out in the open when a tornado approaches. Many people seek refuge below ground in specially designed bunkers when a tornado nears their property.

Question 1: Why would it be dangerous to be caught out in the open with a tornado nearby?

Question 2: Why do people seek refuge below ground when a tornado approaches?

Paragraph Level Non Fiction: *Plants*

One: *Plants*

Plants are of fundamental importance to life. Without plants, many living animals and other organisms would soon fade away and vanish. Higher life forms, including humans, depend on plants for their food and survival. However, many species of plants are capable of making their own food using photosynthesis, which converts sunlight into energy.

Question 1: Would plants survive if there were no animals?

Question 2: What may happen to all plant eating animals in the world if all plants in the world disappeared overnight?

Two: *Seeds*

A seed has within its outer casing the building blocks to create a plant. Each seed has the basic parts of a plant and a small supply of food. The food nourishes the tiny embryo until germination can take place. The remarkable thing is that the seed can remain dormant for a period of months or even years, waiting for the right conditions to grow and thrive.

Question 1: What would happen to a seed if it ran out of food?

Question 2: Would a seed germinate and grow if the conditions made it difficult for the plant to survive?

Three: *Plants converting energy*

Plants are remarkable in that they do not need to find food. In contrast to animals, plants can make their own food. Plants contain a green pigment called chlorophyll (chl-or-o-phyl), which converts the sunlight's energy into a chemical energy. The converted energy is stored as a food source which the plant uses to grow and develop.

Question 1: What might happen to plants if there was no sunlight?

Question 2: Do plants need chlorophyll? How do you know that?

Four: *Pollination*

Pollination is the process where pollen is transferred from plant to plant. Pollen is essential for plant species survival and sexual reproduction. The most common type of pollinators are insects, including honeybees, bumblebees and butterflies. Plants entice insects by using bright colors and sweet nectars.

Question 1: Would a pollinating insect be more attracted to a red rose or a plant that did not flower?

Question 2: Why do you think plants use nectar to attract insects?

Inference Activities

Five: *Venus Flytrap*

Some plants don't just rely on photosynthesis for their food. The Venus flytrap is deadly to unsuspecting insects. To an insect, the Venus flytrap looks to be an attractive plant with the promise of sweet nectar. But the plant's appearance is a trap. The plant waits for the insect to settle on its leaf tip then springs shut, quick as a flash. The plant then later digests the insect.

Question 1: Why do you think the Venus flytrap is designed to have such an attractive look to insects?

Question 2: Why would the leaf tips need to spring shut quickly?

Six: *The Teasel*

Many plants have complex defence systems. A fascinating plant is the Teasel. The Teasel has an unusual construction in that pairs of leaves form together which creates a natural cup. The Teasel defends itself by forming a moat of water at the leaf's base. When snails or insects attempt to climb the leaf, to feed on the leaves, they fall into the moat and drown.

Question 1: Why is the Teasel a fascinating plant?

Question 2: Why would plants need complex defence systems?

Seven: *Cacti*

Cacti are a desert plant that can survive without very much water. Because they live in desert regions, Cacti have evolved unique ways of storing large amounts of water. A feature of their water gathering ability is that cacti have long roots that can collect water from a wide area. Cacti also have effective defence systems such as spines and thorns to discourage grazing animals.

Question 1: Why do cacti store large amounts of water?

Question 2: Why are spines and thorns effective in protecting cacti from grazing animals?

Eight: *Dandelions*

Dandelions have yellow flower heads that eventually form into tufts of tiny fruit that contain seeds of the plant. If you blow on a dandelion's seed head, the seeds are dispersed through the air on their own parachute. The tiny parachute is lifted high in to the air by the wind and carried on a long journey, far from the original plant. The seeds then settle in multiple locations.

Question 1: Why do dandelions rely on the wind to spread their seed?

Question 2: Why is the spread of the dandelion plant difficult to control?

Inference Activities

Nine: *Cultivation*

The cultivation of plants for food crops began many thousands of years ago. When humans made the leap from hunter gatherer to forming settlements, they cultivated plants on an on-going basis. They selected the most nutritious and best growing plants to form crops, and then used the seeds for the following year. In this way, food crops such as rice, wheat and potato could sustain larger and larger populations.

Question 1: Why did early humans use the seeds from current crops the following year?

Question 2: Why did the cultivation of food help to feed large populations of people?

Ten: *Parasitic plants*

Parasitic plants steal food from other organisms rather than making their own. Parasitic plants don't use sunlight to make food. Rather, they are hidden from view and attach themselves to the host plant's roots using a type of sucker. The suckers absorb stored glucose and minerals from the host plant.

Question 1: Do parasitic plants need sunlight to survive? How do you know that?

Question 2: If the host plant died, what might happen to the parasitic plant?

Paragraph Level Non-Fiction: *Solar System*

One: *The Sun*

Our sun is a star. It is so big that its mass could easily contain over a million Earth sized planets. The sun's surface is also incredibly hot. It has a temperature of 5,500 °C. In the sun's core, the temperature reaches a searing 1500,000 °C, which is the temperature at which nuclear reactions occur. The sun bathes the Earth in light and heat.

Question 1: What might it be like on Earth if there were no sun?

Question 2: Is the sun much bigger than the Earth?

Two: *The Earth*

Earth is unique among the planetary bodies in our solar system, because it contains life. The Earth has oceans of liquid water on its surface and vast amounts of oxygen and nitrogen in its atmosphere. It is thought that for life to occur, water needs to be present. Earth has an abundance of various types of life forms, which is related to the amount of water on the planet's surface.

Question 1: Do dry planets such as Venus and Mercury have life?

Question 2: Would Earth have life if it had no water on its surface?

Inference Activities

Three: _Venus_

Venus is the brightest planet in the sky. Venus is a barren planet that is so bright because it is close to the Earth and its thick cloud cover reflects much of the sun's light. In fact, the thick cloud cover acts like a shield that keeps the planet's heat trapped in. The temperature on Venus's surface is 480 °C, which is hot enough to melt lead. Venus contains no oxygen, and its atmosphere contains heavy amounts of the poison gas, carbon dioxide.

Question 1: Would we be able to breathe on Venus's surface without oxygen tanks?

Question 2: Would there be oceans of water on Venus's surface?

Four: _Olympus Mons_

Olympus Mons is a volcano on the surface of Mars. At 25 kilometres high, the volcano is three times the height of Earth's Mt Everest. _Olympus Mons_ is a vast 600 kilometres wide and is the largest mountain in our solar system. The volcano has long been extinct, and is near to a chain of massive volcanoes on Mars's surface known as the _Tharsis Montes_.

Question 1: Does _Olympus Mons_ still erupt? How do you know that?

Question 2: Are there any mountains on Earth which are bigger than _Olympus Mons_? How do you know that?

Five: *Marriner Valley*

Mars's *Valles Marinaris*, or Marriner Valley, is the grandest canyon in the solar system, and dwarfs all other canyons. The canyon is so colossal and so long that it covers a distance of nearly 5000 kilometres. This means the canyon's length is greater than large countries such as Australia and the United States. The valley is also seven kilometres *deep* - as deep as Earth's Mount Everest is tall.

Question 1: Is the Grand Canyon in the United States as big as the *Valles Marinaris*? How do you know that?

Question 2: Would you be able to walk the length of the *Valles Marinaris* in one day? How do you know that?

Six: *The Moon*

The Moon is Earth's satellite. The Moon rotates around the Earth in what is known as a synchronous (syn-chron-ous) orbit. This means that we always see the same face of the moon, or its near side. Though the moon is the brightest object in the night sky, it is in fact very dark, similar to black coal. The moon appears very bright in the night sky due to the Sun's rays reflecting off its dark surface, making it seem as if it glows.

Question 1: Would the moon glow if there was no sun?

Question 2: Do we ever see the moon's far side?

Inference Activities

Seven: *Titan*

Titan is an amazing and frigid moon that orbits the gas giant, Saturn, in the cold regions of the outer solar system. Titan has many similarities to Earth. For instance, like Earth, Titan has a dense atmosphere and many stable bodies of surface liquid. In other words, Titan has lakes and small seas. The seas and lakes do not contain water but liquid hydrocarbon. Also, like Earth, Titan has shorelines, rivers and seasons.

Question 1: Would Titan have a winter, summer or spring?

Question 2: Is it cold on Titan?

Eight: *Europa*

Europa is a moon that orbits the planet Jupiter. Though small, Europa is unique amongst planetary bodies in that it contains a water ocean beneath its icy outer layer. Europa's icy surface is as smooth as a billiard ball and is broken up with long cracks. There is a theory that beneath Europa's icy surface its water oceans may contain life. Due to tidal forces, created by Jupiter's gravity, Europa's water oceans are warm, and perhaps Earth like.

Question 1: Does Europa's surface have mountains?

Question 2: Why is it thought that Europa's oceans may contain life?

Nine: *Io*

Over 400 active volcanoes consistently erupt plumes of sulphur onto Io's (eye- o) surface. Io is a small moon that orbits the huge gas giant, Jupiter. It is the most volcanically active object in the solar system. Io's extreme volcanism is caused by friction created by Jupiter's massive bulk, which produces tidal heating within Io's interior.

Question 1: Would you be able to see the planet Jupiter clearly from Io's surface? How do you know that?

Question 2: Is Io more volcanically active than Earth?

Ten: *Neptune*

Neptune is the eighth planet in our solar system and the planet that is furthest from the sun. Neptune is a deep blue color and is made up of gases. It is known as a gas giant. It has the strongest winds of any planet in the solar system. The fastest winds detected on Neptune have been as high as 2100 kilometres an hour. In comparison, even the most severe storm winds on Earth rarely exceed 250 kilometres an hour.

Question 1: Would it be safe to fly a kite in Neptune's atmosphere?

Question 2: Would the sun be as big in the sky on Neptune as it is on Earth?

Paragraph Level Non-Fiction: *Animal Kingdom*

One: *The Bar-Tailed Godwit*

The Bar-Tailed Godwit is a type of wading bird that is famous for making the longest non-stop migration. Each year the Godwit migrates from the cold state of Alaska all the way down south to New Zealand, a distance of over 11000 kilometres. The Godwit spends the winter in the more temperate environment offered by countries such as New Zealand.

Question 1: Why might the Godwit migrate to the temperate regions of New Zealand at winter time?

Question 2: Does the Godwit stop to rest during its long flight?

Two: *The Colossal Squid*

The Colossal Squid is one of the rarest animals known to man. The squid is famous for its huge size, hence the name colossal. The animal is about 13 meters long. If the squid were to be carved into calamari, the rings would be as big as tractor tires. This deep sea monster is has the largest eyes in the animal kingdom, as big as dinner plates.

Question 1: Have there been many Colossal Squids captured?

Question 2: Would the Colossal Squid have good eyesight?

Three: *The Siberian Tiger*

The Siberian Tiger is the largest cat in the world and can weigh as much as 320 kilograms (710 pounds). The big cat is now an endangered species and is confined in the wild to far eastern Siberia. Tigers rely on power and stealth to capture their prey. This is unlike big cats such as lions, which rely on speed and agility. Each tiger has a uniquely camouflaged striped coat. Tigers are identified by their coats as easily as people are identified by their fingerprints.

Question 1: Would a tiger struggle to capture a fast moving gazelle over open ground? How do you know that?

Question 2: Why would it be difficult to spot a tiger in the jungle?

Four: *Piranha*

The piranha is a legendary small fish with razor sharp teeth found in South American rivers. The fish is famed for eating unwary people who swim in piranha infested waters. Fortunately, the stories about mad feeding frenzies are just that - stories. Though piranhas do occasionally bite people, it is more by mistaken identity than a wilful desire to eat humans.

Question 1: Why do you think piranhas are considered legendary?

Question 2: Why would a piranha's bite be potentially very painful?

Five: *Wandering Albatross*

The bird with the greatest wingspan is the Wandering Albatross. These majestic birds soar high above the world's southern oceans and can travel up to 500 kilometres (270 miles) a day while hunting for food. The Wandering Albatross is built similarly to a glider in that it has a light body but very long and narrow wings. This body shape allows the bird to ride almost effortlessly on wind currents, using small amounts of energy.

Question 1: What food would a Wandering Albatross hunt for?

Question 2: Would a Wandering Albatross be able to glide on wind currents if its wings were short? How do you know that?

Six: *Blue Whale*

The largest animal in Earth's history is the Blue Whale. The whale can grow to a length of 25 metres and weigh as much as 200 tons. A Blue Whale's tongue is enormous and can weigh as much as an African elephant. The massive animal feeds by first gulping down a huge amount of water. The gigantic tongue then blasts the water through very thin baleen plates in its jaw, leaving tiny krill – the whale's diet – behind. The krill is then swallowed.

Question 1: Would a Blue Whale's tongue fit into a car's boot?

Question 2: Is water let out slowly or quickly through the baleen plates? How do you know that?

Seven: *Crocodiles*

Salt water crocodiles are supreme predators and have survived almost unchanged since the time of the dinosaurs. They are considered the predator most likely to eat people. In fact, salt water crocodiles will eat any animal they can manage to get their jaws around. And once they have the animal in their jaws, there's no getting away. Salt water crocodiles can exert a force pressure through their jaws of several tons.

Question 1: Is the salt water crocodile considered a successful predator?

Question 2: Has the salt water crocodile been on Earth for a short time or a long time? How do you know that?

Eight: *Cheetah*

The cheetah's body is built for speed. It has slim, muscular legs, a long tail to help with balance, and unique pads on its paws to help it gain purchase as it powers across the ground. This all makes the cheetah a devastatingly fast animal that can reach speeds of up to 112 km's per hour (70 mph). Though quick, the cheetah is a burst animal that cannot maintain high speeds for long.

Question 1: Can a cheetah pursue an antelope for several hours?

Question 2: What might happen to a cheetah's speed if it lost its tail?

Inference Activities

Nine: *Orang-utan*

Orang-utans are unique in that they are the largest tree dwelling apes, and are highly skilled climbers. Orang-utans are intelligent creatures and have been known to fashion rough tools. For instance, they assemble umbrellas out of large leaves when it rains hard, as it often does in tropical rainforests.

Question 1: Why do orang-utans assemble umbrellas?

Question 2: Do orang-utans have difficulty climbing trees? How do you know that?

Ten: *The black mamba*

The black mamba is a highly dangerous venomous snake in Africa. There are several factors that make the snake so dangerous. For instance, the black mamba is very fast. It can move across the ground at up to 20 km per hour (12 mph), which is impressive as it is essentially crawling on its belly. Also, the snake is very aggressive and will chase people when it's disturbed.

Question 1: Why would it be a bad idea to approach a black mamba?

Question 2: Why is the black mamba such a feared snake?

Text Level Inference

Fiction

Chapter six

Fiction Story *Text Level*

The Witches of Carpathia

The witches dropped from the clear sky like a whirlwind. The witch nearest me screeched harsh incantations in her strange tongue. With one hand she guided the broomstick; with the other she wove a black hammer spell with her spidery fingers, which she unleashed at me.

I ducked low but was not fast enough. The spell struck me full on the side of my helmet, causing it to fly off and clatter noisily down the tower steps. I sank to my knees. I was dimly aware of movement and my fellow tower guards' cries of fear and panic as they fought the strange harpies. Tears clouded my eyes and the world around me blurred and became as mist. 'Get up you fool,' a voice in my head commanded. 'Up!

My legs were like jelly, my head ached terribly and I could taste blood in my mouth, but I stood up. And, as I stood on my tottering legs, I instinctively raised my shield. I was just in time. A witch flew past, inches from my head and hurled a bolt of pure while light. The blast of heat clipped the shield and ricocheted like an arrow glancing off stone, leaving only a scorch mark. The sound of it filled my ears, but I was unhurt.

Inference Activities

I held the *Gorgan* sword in my left hand and peered over the edge of my shield. There were three witches, not 10 feet distant, who hovered easily on their broomsticks and watched me with their fierce eyes. I had time to observe their savage, yet delicate features, and long flowing hair. The witches were like finely honed steel blades from *Mithrond*: cold, deadly and beautiful.

The other tower guards had fled. I alone stood and faced the menace. I was doomed unless help arrived, or I managed to make it to the relative safety of the tower stairs. The witches readied their assault upon me while I narrowed my gaze and inched slowly back to the stairs...

Inference Questions – The Witches of Carpathia

One

Is this story a fantasy story? How do you know that?

Two

According to the main character, the witches were like finely honed steel blades. What did he mean?

Three

The character describes his legs as being like gelatin. What did he mean?

Four

Whose voice was in the character's head? How do you know that?

Five

Was the character up high in the castle or standing in the castle's courtyard? How do you know that?

Six

Were the witches confident in their abilities? How do you know that?

Seven

Why did the other guards flee? How do you know that?

Eight

Why was the character inching slowly back to the stairs?

Nine

When the blast of heat clips the character's shield, does it make much of a noise? How do you know that?

Ten

Are the witches' fingers long and slender, or short and fat? How do you know that?

Text Level Inference

Non-Fiction

Chapter six

Newspaper Article *Text Level*

China to Launch Second Lunar Probe

China's second lunar probe is predicted to be dispatched into space November next year. The operation is part of a joint project with the more advanced Russian space program and comes after a two-year delay, a source reported Tuesday.

The probe, K10 - F, was due to launch in October 2018 with Russia's rocket "Cosmic Dancer" from Uzbekistan but the mission was initially cancelled, the official Chinese state news media reported.

An unidentified source revealed that the probe is due to search the lunar surface with its main focus being to investigate suitable areas for any future base building on the lunar surface.

China has already begun probing the moon surface with its moon orbiter and this will be the next step in its determined and inspired space exploration timetable. Its stated aim is to eventually, in future, be able to compete with the United States NASA program.

The report added that China has plans to propel a Sun probe independently sometime in 2012. At present, China have plans for its probe – tentatively titled Solar 2 – to orbit and complete a number of important tests in preparation for a possible solar space station.

Inference Activities

China is only the world's third nation - without assistance from other nations - to independently launch a human into space.

Inference Questions - China to Launch Second Probe

One

Is this China's first lunar probe to be launched?

Two

According to the report, is China definitely going to launch its probe in November next year?

Three

Has China built any bases before on the lunar surface?

Four

Is China's current space program as big or as successful as NASA's space program?

Five

When China launches its sun probe will it be in partnership with other nations?

Six

China is the third nation to launch a person into space; which are the other two possible countries?

Appendix

Answer Section

Inference from Pictures and Text

'We flew to the ruined and deserted city.'

a.   There are ruined buildings and the place looks deserted

b.   A plane needs a runway to land safely. There are no runways in a city.

c.   It would be very cold being high in the atmosphere in an open cockpit.

'When the ship's captain looked through the telescope, at the fast approaching vessel, he gasped in fear.'

a.   The sailors are pirates. The ship has a skull and crossbones pirate flag.

b.   The captain would be fearful of pirates because they are dangerous and murderous.

c.   From the past. The vintage of the ship suggests 17th – 18th century C.E.

'I got the shock of my life when the train left the tracks and became airborne.'

a.   Trains don't leave the track and don't fly. It would be a huge surprise to be on one that flew.

b.   It's science fiction because flying trains are fantastical and not from real life.

c.   Trains only require track to travel from place to place and don't need wings.

'The space trooper calmly looked through his range finder. The fierce alien warriors were right behind him.'

a.   The trooper is being chased by fierce aliens so he is in some danger.

b.   He's a space trooper so he works in outer space.

110

c.   The space trooper is calm so he sounds very competent and confident.

"Take me to your leader," said the creature'

a.   The creature has big eyes on long stems. His vision must be amazingly good.

b.   The creature is certainly an alien and is not from Earth. There is nothing on Earth like this.

c.   The creature's vision is advanced. We can assume the creature needs good vision on its home world.

'Peter expertly launched the rocket and was thrilled with its speed and power.'

a.   Peter is thrilled with the rocket, which indicates he's having fun.

b.   Peter is high above the city so he is up very high.

c.   Peter is described as expert, so he is in control of the rocket.

'I needed to get the clothes off the clothesline. I didn't have much time.'

a.   It's about to pour rain.

b.   The clothes will get wet and possibly damaged by the approaching storm.

c.   The clouds are massing and the first drops are falling. The storm is imminent.

'Adam had been warned to never sit in grandpa's chair. Now it was too late.'

a.   The chair was potentially dangerous. Especially if you were to fall out while it was flying.

b.   The chair is flying and possibly out of control. Adam looks frightened.

c.   No. Adam is flying above the rooftops.

When Captain Perry felt water tickling over his toes, he knew he was in trouble. He pushed the "to surface" button.'

a.   Inferring from his suit Captain Perry is deep in the ocean depths.

b.   Water entering the suit is potentially disastrous. Ne needs to get to the surface quickly.

c.   No. The complexity of the suit and the odd fish indicates deep sea diving.

'Kathy leaned forward and guided Saladin over. Only one obstacle to go and the gold medal was hers.'

a.   Saladin is the horse Kathy is riding.

b.   Kathy is in a competition because she is competing for a gold medal.

c.   Kathy leaned forward to make jumping the horse easier and safer.

Chapter Two

Sentence Level

Concept: Location

One: The passenger jet is at the airport.

Two: Sasha is at the zoo

Three: The goat is on a mountain.

Four: On an iceberg or the Antarctic.

Five: In the cockpit of an jet aircraft.

Six: In a car.

Seven: In the classroom.

Eight: On the banks of a river.

Nine: In a private or public pool.

Ten: In a dentist's chair.

Eleven: In a cinema.

Twelve: In the schoolyard.

Concept: Time

One: Chloe had been holding the ice-cream for a while because it is dripping over her hand.

Two: Early morning. The sun is just starting to rise.

About 3:00 – 3:30 pm.

Three: Early evening. The day was warm and is now cooling, which indicates the sun has gone down.

Four: About 10-15 minutes to wait for the soup to cool. (Answers will vary)

Five: Post office usually opens at 9:00 am, so we could say it was 8:00 – 8:30 am.

Six: Christmas – December.

Seven: Karen is swimming in the evening.

Eight: Milk takes about 10- 15 minutes to boil over. (Answers will vary)

Nine: Winter

Ten: Late afternoon, early evening.

Concept: What

One: passenger jet airliner.

Two: Peter's pushbike.

Three: The zoo.

Four: His skin.

Five: A telescope.

Six: A volcano erupting.

Seven: A hot dry place. A desert.

Eight: A fossil embedded in rock.

Nine: A banana.

Ten: A spider.

Eleven: Jasper is a horse.

Twelve: A submarine.

Concept: Who

One: A policeman

Two: The baby's mother (Answers may vary)

Three: Classroom teacher.

Four: The chef.

Five: Mr Harris is an electrician.

Six: A nurse or doctor.

Seven: Phillip is a truck driver.

Eight: Natasha is a hairdresser

Nine: Jesse is a fireman.

Ten: Mr. Martin is a bus driver.

Eleven: Andrew is a dairy farmer.

Twelve: Helen is a Parking Inspector.

Concept: Why

One: The sheep got out through the open gate.

Two: It had been snowing throughout the night.

Three: The DVD player wasn't plugged in so there was nothing to power it.

Four: Jenny needed air for when she was underwater.

Five: They were supporting the local team.

Six: The storm had ripped the power lines down.

Seven: The dog was barking at the cat, which was invading his territory.

Eight: Adam had a flat tire.

Nine: To cut the grass; which had grown long.

Ten: The kitchen was full of smoke and needed airing out.

Eleven: It was very cold once the girl got out of the pool.

Twelve: The chef didn't like the taste of the stew.

Chapter Three

Paragraph Level: Science Fiction and Fantasy

One

1) Yes. The tower is bathed in the moon's light indicating night-time.

2) Yes. His hearts thumps wildly.

Two

1) Spike is a robot or android of some type. He has artificial limbs.

2) 20 minutes.

Three

1) It's a time machine. It travels through a time portal to specific times in history.

2) A Roman outfit would not be suited to the 18th century.

Four

1) No. All he has are his bare hands.

2) The passage was the only way he could get to his ship and off the planet.

Five

1) No, unlikely. There is no such thing as a brundle trumper on Earth.

2) Threes sets of jaws indicates three heads.

Six

1) Probably a dragon.

2) No, the castle is described as abandoned.

Seven

1) Jenson is a horse because the character is mounted on a beast that trots.

2) The character is waiting for the gates to open so he can confront the evil lord.

Eight

1) Some type of bird. Feathers left behind indicate it was a bird.

2) The farmer is angry because his prized soup was spread across the floor.

Nine

1) To open the gates from the inside.

2) A bow and arrow.

Ten

1) The wizard used some type of energy/electrical bolt as a weapon.

2) The blast knocked the character off his feet.

Chapter Four

Paragraph Level: Myths and Legends

One

1) No. Prometheus was immortal, which means he lives for ever.

2) Zeus was vengeful and condemned Prometheus to eternal suffering, so yes he was angry.

Two

1) Yes. Pandora was warned to never open the jar and when she did she loosed evil into the world.

2) Pandora was very curious and couldn't resist looking.

Three

1) The Minotaur was brutal and aggressive.

2) The Minotaur was in a complex maze, which made it difficult to locate.

Four

1) Thor's strength would be cut by half.

2) Thor striking enemies with his hammer causes thunder according to the myth.

Five

1) The infants would probably have perished.

2) A harsh environment is a place where you could not expect to survive long without assistance of some kind.

Six

1) No. Maui needed long hair to create rope.

2) Yes, according to the myth the sun now travels slowly across the horizon.

Seven

1) The crow was greedy and didn't share the days catch with the hawk.

2) Probably not, but may have had bad luck. (Answers will vary)

Eight

1) Galahad was able to find the grail because he was pure of heart.

2) No. It took many knights many fruitless years to find the grail.

Nine

1) The lion's skin was too thick for the sword and spear to penetrate.

2) Heracles is described as being very strong. He was too strong for the lion.

Ten

1) No. The phoenix is described as being a mythical bird.

2) Yes. The phoenix must be colorful because its feathers contain all the known colors.

Chapter Five

Paragraph Level: Adventure

On

1) The weather was a storm at sea. The wind was howling and the waves were gigantic.

2) Yes, the character is described as hanging on to the mast for dear life.

Two

1) Old Boxy is a wily and moody old horse. Stirrup and saddle and riding indicate a horse.

2) Yes. All the people flock to watch the character ride the horse. So Old Boxy is well known.

Three

1) Probably a jet fighter of some kind. Something which is powerful enough to reach the upper atmosphere.

2) Yes the pilot is being described as being in the upper atmosphere and being able to see entire continents.

Four

1) Rocketgirl's feet were moving so fast it was difficult to see them.

2) No. She would need a lot of speed to be able to jump such a distance.

Five

1) The character is climbing a mountain.

2) Yes. High altitude and high winds with lots of ice and snow would be freezing.

Six

1) Yes. The guards switched on the light switch, and the flash in the dark room also alerted the guards.

2) Yes, the character is highly trained indicating he/she does this as a profession.

Seven

1) Yes, words such as gallop thunder indicate speed and the character leant forward in the saddle to ease wind resistance at high speed.

2) Phantom is a horse. Words such as saddle, reins and gallop indicate a horse.

Eight

1) Yes, it took two months to find the valley.

2) Exotic species refers to rare or unknown plants and animals.

Nine

1) A submarine. It's a ship that is underwater and descending under the water.

2) The depth charges are explosives that are designed to crush a submarine's hull. The impact of a nearby explosion would shake the entire ship violently and you would need to hold onto something tightly.

Ten

1) Andrew was following a treasure map. The treasure's location was marked with a black cross.

2) It was hard work digging a hole in such difficult ground.

Chapter Six

Paragraph Level: Whimsy

One

1) The boy is inferring his grandmother is a wicked old witch.

) No, he states that his grandmother was faster than him.

Two

1) Social graces might be greetings such as 'How are you?' or 'You look well,' etc.

2) Uncle Angus is too big and strong.

Three

1) Jed doesn't learn from his mistakes and continues to be manipulated by the cat.

2) Jed would like revenge against being tormented by the cat.

Four

1) He needed to get the pick axe to hack through all the ice.

2) No the clothes come out 3 sizes smaller indicating it doesn't work properly.

Five

1) He had found the keys.

2) Yes. He had clothes and pizza boxes scattered throughout the room.

Six

1) The children got caught in a downpour.

2) Sally though they could reach the safety of the supermarket before it started to pour rain.

Seven

1) Derek was standing in the plane's doorway.

2) Derek was skydiving with a parachute.

Eight

1) The character's deepest fear is the dentist's drill.

2) No, because the brother now increases the character's fear and anxiety.

Nine

1) Yes, the character bounds up the stairs to his room.

2) A child playacting. He is using ordinary pyjamas as a super suit.

Ten

1) No. The bully ate the sandwich in the belief that it contained jam.

2) The chili was burning the poor boy's tongue and mouth which is most unpleasant.

Chapter Seven

Paragraph Level: Kid's Stuff

One

1) Yes. The character describes the chip as an explosion of flavor.

2) The character is holding chips.

Two

1) The character knew he was about to be blamed for using his sister's hairbrush as a dog brush.

2) The character infers he used the brush when he states 'the dog's brush was nowhere to be found…I used the first thing I could find.'

Three

1) Ice-cream, which is in a glass freezer and gets put into a waffle cone.

2) All the colors of the rainbow and other colors indicate there were many different flavors to choose from.

Four

1) A bus.

2) The character thought he/she had a chance of catching the bus before it got away.

Five

1) Grandma didn't want to waste any part of the food.

2) No. The character dreads the feeling of getting the core stuck between the teeth.

Six

1) Yes, they had been playing for ages, or what seemed an age.

2) The character has a better chance of rolling 3-6 than 1-2. He has better odds.

Seven

1) The character counted the 12 chimes of the grandfather clock.

2) He was walking in the dark and couldn't see the sideboard.

Eight

1) The character saw how high up he was.

2) Because the character was taking so long and they wanted their turn.

Nine

1) No, he's fifth in line.

2) Because the boy is drinking slowly and the character is desperate for a drink.

Ten

1) No, the Aunt grew the cucumber in her garden.

2) The mother was embarrassed by her son's rude behaviour.

Chapter Eight

Paragraph Level: History

One

1) No. Henry Ford was the first to mass produce cars on an assembly line.

2) It was both cheap to buy and run.

Two

1) Napoleon's armies had had many victories before

2) No. Napoleon was sent into exile and never returned to France.

Three

1) The printing press enabled books to be printed easily, making them affordable and widely read.

2) Each book had to be written by hand, which would be hard work and take forever.

Four

1) No. Ancient Egyptian writing was too complex and too weird to understand.

2) The translator used several different writings of the same message to translate the unknown writing style.

Five

1) It would be dark because there were few windows.

2) No. Modern homes generally have lots of natural light and good ventilation.

Six

1) The armor was bulky and it was easy to lose balance when riding a horse.

2) The stirrup gave stability and balance to the rider allowing him to carry heavier equipment.

Seven

1) The Sumerians wrote their language onto clay tablets which can survive over intact for many years.

2) They were able to record transactions much more quickly and reliably.

Eight

1) Marco Polo travelled on foot, which means he travelled very slowly.

2) For safety. There is safety in numbers.

Nine

1) The king was uncaring and raised taxes.

2) He wanted to raise taxes on the poor but not the rich.

Ten

1) The Titanic sank on its first voyage so it was not unsinkable.

2) The Titanic only made the one voyage, its first voyage.

Four

Paragraph Level: Weather

One

1) Beneath 20 degrees it starts to get cold.

2) Above 25 degrees people are looking to cool down. Water is best for this.

Two

1) No. Fog absorbs sound, making it harder to hear.

2) You can't see more than a few meters in front. Reaction time to danger would be compromised.

Three

1) Both skyscrapers and storm clouds are very high.

2) You may get struck by lightning or hit by debris.

Four

1) After.

2) Thunder can be a very loud and sudden noise and can easily wake people.

Five

1) Ice crystals are very light and so cannot fall through the air.

2) They would melt.

Six

1) It may shatter and be destroyed.

2) Cyclones need heat created by warm ocean currents. Land doesn't produce enough heat.

Seven

1) There is nothing to hold the soil down.

2) All life relies on abundant water. If there is scarce water many plants and animals would perish from dehydration.

Eight

1) Weather is very changeable and random.

2) Maybe. (Answers will vary)

Nine

1) No. They need to become large before droplets form rain.

2) Yes. Hail is frozen water, so it must be cold in the clouds.

Ten

1) Because tornados cause extensive damage and are deadly.

2) Because it is driven by wind, a tornado has difficulty damaging anything below ground.

Chapter Nine

Paragraph Level: Plants

One

1) Yes. Plants don't need animals to survive. They have photosynthesis.

) They would all soon perish.

Two

1) The seed would die.

2) No. The seed would wait for the right conditions.

Three

1) Plants need sunlight to create photosynthesis. Without sunlight plants may die.

2) Yes. Without chlorophyll no energy could be converted.

Four

1) To a red rose because it is attractive to the insect.

2) Insects love nectar, which is why plants use it to attract insects.

Five

1) An insect wouldn't go near a Venus flytrap if it thought it deadly. It thinks the plant is a normal flower with the promise of nectar.

2) Flies and other insects have quick reflexes.

Six

1) It's unusual because it forms a natural moat to kill insects.

2) They are constantly in danger of being eaten by insects and animals.

Seven

1) There may be long periods of time without rain.

2) The spines make it too painful and awkward for animals to eat cacti.

Eight

1) Wind carries the seed to multiple random locations increasing the chance of the plant's reproduction and survival.

2) Because the spreading of the seed is so random. The plant can grow in multiple locations at once.

Nine

1) They would have a guaranteed crop and food source the following year.

2) The food was easy to grow and plentiful.

Ten

1) No. They use other plants' food sources.

2) The parasitic plant would also die because its food source is gone.

Chapter Ten

Paragraph Level – Solar System

One

1) The Earth would be a frozen dark place with no life.

2. Yes. The sun can contain over a million earth sized planets in its mass.

Two

1) No. Neither planet contains water, so they cannot sustain life.

2) Unlikely. If there was no water its not likely there would be life on Earth.

Three

1) No. Its atmosphere would be poisonous to us and we would die.

2) No. Any water Venus may have had evaporated billions of years ago. It's too hot.

Four

1) No. It is extinct, which means it's dead.

2) No Mount Everest is Earth's highest mountain and Olympus Mons is three times higher than Everest.

Five

1) No. The Valles Marinaris is as wide as the United States. The Grand Canyon is a small fraction of its size.

2) No. It would take several months or even years to walk from one end of the valley to the other.

Six

1) No. The moon is black coal and would be terribly dark without the sun's rays reflection off it.

2) No. The same side always faces Earth. The Apollo Mission astronauts are the only people to have seen the moon's far side, or dark side.

Seven

1) Yes. Titan is similar to Earth in that it has seasons.

2) Titan is described as a frigid moon, which means it's extremely cold.

Eight

1) No. Europa's surface is very smooth, like a billiard ball.

2) Europa may contain warm water oceans similar to Earth, which are necessary for life to generate.

Nine

1) Yes. Io is very close to the massive planet Jupiter, and the planet would dominate its horizon.

2) Yes. It is the most volcanically active object in the solar system.

Ten

1) No. It would be impossible for any number of reasons.

2) No. Neptune is much further from the Sun than Earth is, so would look much smaller on Neptune.

Chapter Eleven

Paragraph Level – Animal Kingdom

One

1) The Godwit would not survive the Alaskan winter.

2) No. It flies non-stop.

Two

1) No. They are extremely rare. Only 1 or 2 have been seen and captured.

2) Yes. It has huge eyes.

Three

1) Yes. A gazelle would be too swift. The tiger relies on stealth and power which would be of little use on open ground.

2) The tiger is heavily camouflaged making it difficult to see.

Four

1) The piranha is legendary because it is famed for eating people and animals in a matter of minutes.

2) The piranha's teeth are razor sharp, like a very sharp knife.

Five

1) It is an ocean hunter, so mainly it would hunt for fish and crustaceans.

2) If the albatross's wings were short it would not be able to glide and would need to continually flap its wings to maintain altitude.

Six

1) No. The tongue weighs over 200 tons so it would be far larger than any car boot.

2) The water is blasted out, so the water is let out quickly.

Seven

1) Yes. It has survived unchanged for over 65 million years. It's a very successful species of animal.

2) It has been on Earth for a very long time, far longer than most other species of plants and animals.

Eight

1) No. The cheetah is a burst animal and quickly tires.

2) If a cheetah lost its tail it would lose its balance and fall over when running.

Nine

1) They become uncomfortable when it pours and need some form of shelter.

2) No. Orang-utans are known as skilful climbers.

Ten

1) Black Mamba's are highly dangerous, poisonous and aggressive.

2) It is very fast and very aggressive.

Chapter Twelve

Text Level Story: The Witches of Carpathia

1) Yes, there is a lot of evidence it is a fantasy story. The first piece of evidence is a witch flying on a broomstick hurling spells is fictional. The second are the names for places and objects, such as Mithrond, Gorgan, etc. This tells us the setting is a fantasy world.

2) The character is making an analogy comparing the physical and spiritual attributes of the witches with sharp knives. The character makes the comparison

because he is impressed with the witches strength and beauty, which he believes is similar to a beautifully made knife.

3) The character's legs were wobbly and a bit unstable which is very similar to jelly. He is unstable because he is groggy after getting hit in the head by the witch's spell.

4) The voice is the character's own voice. We know this because the voice is described as being in his head and there were no other characters standing near to him when he was hit by the spell.

5) The character is up high in some form of tower because the tower steps are mentioned.

6) We can infer the witches are confident by their appearance and the character's reaction to them, and the fact that the tower guards have been defeated by them. The witches must be highly competent and confident to achieve that.

7) The guards were panicking as the main character slumped to his knees. We can infer that they bolted soon after.

8) The character was inching back to the stairs so as not to reveal his strategy to the witches who were watching him closely. The character wanted to reach the safety of the stairs before the witches could work out what he was doing.

9) Yes, we can infer that the noise was very loud because it was described as filling the character's ears.

10) We can infer the witches fingers are long and slender because the witches are compared to a steel blade and their fingers are described as spidery, indicating thin and long.

Chapter Thirteen

Newspaper Article: Text Level

1) No, it will be China's second lunar probe to be launched.

2) No, it's only a prediction.

3) No.

4) No, not as yet. They one day hope to be able to compete with NASA in future.

5) Yes, with Russia.

6) The other countries mentioned in the article are Russia and the United States.

About the Author

David Newman is speech-language pathologist and sometime writer who lives and works in Victoria, Australia.

David self publishes books and workbooks to help school-age children acquire language and literacy skills. Starting from scratch, David's popular website - **speech-language-resources.com** - has hundreds of user-friendly webpages and a wealth of free programs, games and guides to assist teachers, parents and speech-language pathologists improve children's speech, and their oral and written language skills.

David is a full-time speech-language pathologist working in Victorian schools. He writes workbooks mostly in his spare time often curled up on the couch cradling a laptop huddled near a gas heater sipping cups of hot tea or playing with his baby son, Michael.

If you found this book helpful or valuable, please let me know by posting a positive **review** for it on **Amazon.com**.

www.speechlanguage-resources.com

Printed in Great Britain
by Amazon